bonsai

a hamlyn care manual

Colin Lewis

Publishing Director
Laura Bamford
Executive Editor
Julian Brown
Assistant Editor
Karen O'Grady
Executive Art Editor
Mark Winwood
Art Director
Keith Martin
Photography
Peter Myers
and Michael Gomez
Production Controller
Melanie Frantz
Picture Research: Liz Fowler

First published in
Great Britain in 1997
by Hamlyn
an imprint of Reed International
Books Limited
Michelin House, 81 Fulham Road,
London SW3 6RB
and Auckland, Melbourne,
Singapore and Toronto

Produced by Mandarin Offset
Printed in China

Contents

APPENDIX
118

WHILE YOU ARE AWAY
120

OUTDOOR BONSAI
IN WINTER
121

TOOLS
122

INTRODUCTION
6

GLOSSARY
123

SO WHAT IS A
BONSAI?
10

INDEX
127

BUYING A BONSAI
20

ACKNOWLEDGEMENTS
128

HOW A TREE WORKS
30

LIGHT, WATER
AND AIR
38

LIFE IN A POT
44

KEEPING IN TRIM
58

TREE DIRECTORY
70

Introduction

For most people, their first encounter with bonsai is probably in a department store or garden nursery during the pre-Christmas shopping panic. Each year many thousands of little trees are imported from China, Japan and other far-eastern countries to satisfy the gift market. Sadly. most of these will die – either through neglect or, ironically, more often through excessive care by their enthusiastic new owners. This fact is all the more sad because the initial disappointment often deters the novice from progressing further, and an opportunity to develop a thoroughly rewarding and satisfying new hobby is lost.

In fact, keeping a bonsai alive and healthy is not significantly more difficult than caring for any other potted plant, provided you understand the difference between an ordinary plant pot and a shallow bonsai container, and you are aware of the requirements of the particular species in question. The watering, feeding and pruning of bonsai are straightforward gardening techniques which can be learnt easily and quickly, even by someone with no prior experience of dealing with plants.

The practical skills required to maintain and develop the shape of a bonsai are also very easy to acquire. Pruning roots and branches, pinching out growing shoots and shaping branches with wire are all simple techniques which are identical to those employed by the most revered Japanese masters. Once learnt they are never forgotten and will enable you to progress your bonsai hobby as far as you want.

Of course, you may well be content with just one or two bonsai to decorate your home or garden. But the chances are that you will be so fascinated by the challenge and reward of cultivating miniaturised trees that you will, in time, become totally hooked. Your collection will grow and your thirst for more detailed and advanced knowledge will grow with it. You may seek the advice of more experienced bonsaiists you meet at your local nursery, or you may subscribe to some of the specialist magazines that are now available. But by far the best way to progress is to join a local club or study group.

Bonsai clubs provide their members with visiting teachers, lecturers, practical workshops, libraries and many other learning aids. But the most valuable asset of all is the contact you will have with other like-minded bonsai enthusiasts of all levels of ability and experience. They will always be ready to offer advice and guidance and, before you know it, you too will be advising new members who come to their first meeting bursting with questions.

One final point. It is always worth remembering that even the top Japanese and Chinese bonsai masters were once beginners themselves, ignorant of the techniques this art form requires. Many of them had to learn the hard way – through trial and error, and by experiment. Their wisdom has been passed on to others, in the East and the West, and is now available to you through the pages of this book, enabling you to gain the knowledge you will need quickly and easily.

Colin Lewis

So what is a bonsai?

To some a bonsai is a cruelly stunted tree confined in a too-small pot. To others it is a work of art resulting from many years of patient care and attention. To the vast majority, it is a fascinating miniature representation of a natural tree form providing its owner with year-round interest and an extremely satisfying pastime.

So, what is a bonsai?

Perhaps it is better to start by explaining what a bonsai is not. A bonsai is not a genetically dwarfed plant, it is not treated with magic potions to reduce its size and, above all, it is not kept small by cruelty in any way. In fact, given an adequate supply of water, air, light and nutrients, a properly maintained bonsai should outlive a full-size tree of the same species (*see Chapter Three*).

Literally translated from Japanese, the term 'bonsai' means a tree in a pot. But over the centuries the definition has come to mean a lot more. To begin with, the tree and the pot form a single harmonious unit where the shape, texture and colour of one compliments the other. Then the tree must be shaped. It is not enough just to plant a tree in a pot and allow nature to take its course – the result would look nothing like a tree and would be very short-lived. Every branch and twig of a bonsai is shaped or eliminated until the chosen image is achieved. From then on, the image is maintained and improved by a constant regime of pruning and trimming.

At all times, a bonsai must be kept in perfect condition. A bonsai can't outgrow an infestation of aphids in the same way a wild tree can. Neither can it send out long roots to search for water in periods of dry weather, and it doesn't receive a regular supply of nutrients from animals and decaying vegetation. A bonsai depends entirely on its current owner for all these things. But don't be deterred; it is not as difficult as it sounds. Remember the literal meaning of bonsai – a tree in a pot. Although a little more time-consuming, a modest bonsai should be no more difficult to care for than any other type of pot plant.

In The Beginning...

Mankind has been growing plants in containers for thousands of years, normally for culinary or medicinal purposes but only very rarely for their beauty. When plants were containerized for decoration it was because of their flowers or foliage. But on one occasion, probably in China, a new concept was born – that of creating miniature representations of natural landscapes in containers. Wall paintings dating back to the Han dynasty, around 200 BC, show such landscapes, complete with trees, rocks and grasses, being carried by servants. Nowadays, over 2,000 years later, these *penjing* still constitute a major part of bonsai culture in China and other far-eastern countries.

There are many legends about the spiritual significance of penjing, most involving powerful emperors or fiery dragons. One favourite suggests that an overweight emperor found travelling tiresome, so he demanded that a miniature replica of his empire should be built in his courtyard to enable him to survey his entire domain from the bedroom window. We shall never know the truth, but it certainly is true that for hundreds of years ownership of a miniature containerized landscape was a considerable status symbol.

The practice of growing single specimen trees in pots came later, again in China, but exactly when is a mystery. These early specimens displayed sparse foliage and rugged, gnarled trunks which often looked like animals or birds. These were called *pun-sai*, the root of the Japanese word *bonsai*, and were the forerunners of the million or more small, commercial 'indoor bonsai' exported from China each year.

**Opposite:
The shape of the white pine bonsai and the decoration on the pot indicate the strong Chinese influence in Japanese culture of this period**

Bonsai in Japan

During the 11th and 12th centuries there was considerable cultural movement between China and its neighbours, particularly the Japanese who readily adopted much of Chinese art and philosophy. Perhaps the most significant influence was the Chinese Zen religion, whose monks played a leading role in introducing bonsai to the Japanese ruling classes.

Bonsai rapidly became entrenched in Japanese culture and seems to have been practiced both on a spiritual and aesthetic level. While the Buddhist monks adopted the intellectual, abstract approach, there is considerable evidence that as early as the late 13th century stunted wild trees were collected and trained as bonsai by ordinary citizens. Specialist techniques also began to develop at this time, although, as the poet Yoshida Kenko suggested in his *Essays in Idleness, c.* 1330, the results were not always successful and tended towards deformity rather than beauty. He regarded bonsai as unnatural and once compared them to beggars with twisted limbs. The same argument continues to rage today, wherever bonsai are grown.

Right: This zelkova, otherwise known as the Grey bark elm (*Zelkova serrata*) already looks like a miniature tree, yet it won't cost a fortune

Below: A Japanese master at work

Development of modern bonsai

Bonsai, like all leisure activities, has been subjected to changes in fashion over the years. For example in the mid-17th century the passion was for camellias, then azaleas. Each year new varieties were exhibited at the equivalent of modern flower shows. One document records 162 new varieties of azalea and 200 camellias. At one point the obsession with variegated plants was so strong that the artistic approach

Above: Specimen Japanese black pine in all its glory. Trees of this stature are quite expensive and are for serious collectors only!

Left: The Japanese characters for 'bonsai' are still identical to the Chinese

to bonsai was almost completely lost in the frantic search for new leaf patterns and colours.

However, it survived, and during the Edo period (1603-1868) became truly established as a highly refined artistic discipline. The techniques became ritualized and the shapes and placement of the branches and trunks governed by a very strict code. Several manuals were produced detailing the exact requirements of the ideal bonsai and giving extremely precise horticultural instructions.

By the late 19th century bonsai had become an industry, with many professional artists and commercial growers supplying an ever-increasing demand

Bonsai in the West

There are records of early Victorian travellers returning from the Orient telling stories of bizarre little trees, with intentionally bent and twisted branches, apparently clinging to life in ceramic containers. But it was not until the Paris Exhibition in 1878 that bonsai were appreciated by the western public. The display in the Japanese Pavilion won a gold medal and brought bonsai to the attention of the European middle classes.

Classic Japanese bonsai follow clearly defined styles which are based on idealized images of natural tree-forms. The story each one tells is of the tree itself and the environment it lives in.

at all levels of society. In 1892 the first Artistic Bonsai Concourse was held in a Tokyo restaurant, and in 1928 the first of the current series of Kokufu-ten exhibitions was held in the Metropolitan Art Museum in Tokyo.

Japanese and Chinese styles

While bonsai in Japan was undergoing centuries of development and refinement which was producing increasingly simplified and, to the westerner, arguably more aesthetic results, in China the only significant change was that bonsai became more populist in its appeal. There are a great number of myths and legends surrounding Chinese bonsai, and the grotesque or animal-like trunks and root formations are still highly prized today. Chinese bonsai come from the landscape of the imagination and images of fiery dragons and coiled serpents take far greater precedence over images of trees.

Above: The animal-like roots of this Sageretia are typical of Chinese specimen bonsai

Right: This little pistachio would be a good, inexpensive tree for the novice to learn on

Ironically, it was as a result of World War Two that bonsai became the internationally popular pastime it is today. Servicemen and diplomats returning from tours of duty in Japan brought back examples as souvenirs. Some people took time to learn about their care before leaving Japan and a few of these original imports are still alive today. In the United States the large ex-patriot Japanese population in California provided the vital link between the energetic, enthusiastic westerner with time on his hands and the traditional Japanese wisdom built over the centuries.

Nowadays bonsai is practiced all over the world, and the different cultures, climates and species of each country have prompted the development of new styles and techniques. The Port Jackson figs of Australia, the American buttonwood and the Scots pines of Europe all have distinct natural styles that are echoed in their bonsai forms, and particular horticultural idiosyncrasies that required the development of appropriate new techniques. Local clubs are formed by groups of enthusiasts, keen to help each other learn. Each year there are many local, national and international conventions and seminars where amateurs and professionals gather to exhibit their trees and to increase their knowledge.

For centuries potted trees, like the flowering apricots pictured here, have been used in China to greet visitors to family residences and important buildings

Commercial bonsai

For most of us bonsai is not a quest for artistic fulfilment or a scientific challenge: it is simply a rewarding and creative pastime.

Our first encounter with bonsai was probably in a local garden centre or department store, where modest little trees are on sale for not-so-modest prices. Sadly, the high price seldom reflects a tree's artistic merit but is due more to the fact that producing a bonsai is a time-consuming and labour-intensive operation, and then it has to be shipped halfway round the world!

Indoor bonsai

Ironically, although it was the Japanese who introduced bonsai to the west and first opened up the market here, the majority of commercial bonsai sold in the west today are produced in China. For one thing, there is no shortage of labour or space in China. But more importantly, the Chinese traditionally use sub-tropical or tropical species which, in temperate climates, need extra protection during winter. Furthermore, unlike hardy species, they can be kept indoors all year round if

need be, making them ideally suited to flat-dwellers and this way their appeal is broadened to the non gardener.

The Chinese were very quick to seize the opportunity to exploit the west's growing fascination with bonsai and set up large-scale nurseries to produce vast quantities of relatively cheap trees. At this low end of the range the plants are little more than two-or three-year old rooted cuttings that have been hard pruned once to induce a mass of new shoots prior to export. One person can prune up to a thousand plants in a day.

Medium-priced Chinese bonsai may often feature a clay figure or pagoda glued to a stone somewhere in the pot, but this is just the producer's idea of what appeals to westerners and should be discarded if not to your taste. The trees themselves, however, will have much more to offer. They are older, probably field-grown plants that have been hard pruned. The new growth is shaped with wire or ties and allowed to grow for a season before being pruned again. Then they are regularly trimmed for another year or more before eventually being potted up ready for export.

A typical Japanese bonsai nursery, where plants are meticulously cared for and kept in perfect health

As the trees increase in price the true Chinese styles begin to emerge, and the more expensive specimens are likely to be truly authentic and full of Chinese magic. These are invariably collected from the wild, and can be extremely old. They are styled and refined for a number of years before being offered to overseas buyers. But even at this level, the Chinese make little effort to disguise the evidence of the hand of man. Saw cuts and pruned branches are allowed either to heal or to decay at nature's whim. It's as if the human intervention is just another episode of the tree's natural history.

Other far-eastern countries such as Taiwan and Korea are beginning to take large shares of the 'indoor' bonsai market, concentrating on the low-to medium-priced trees – older, specimen bonsai from these sources are rare. Mediterranean countries like Italy and Israel also produce small sub-tropical bonsai, mostly olives, pistachio, pomegranate and the like. These can be a source of interesting material on which to work but, size for size, rarely have the charm or character of far-eastern trees.

Outdoor bonsai

In spite of indoor bonsai's more popular appeal, once hooked, the bonsai enthusiast invariably turns to hardy species. A collection of hardy bonsai, living in the open, rewards its owner with all the changes in colour and texture associated with the seasons. Your work schedule will also be dictated by the seasons, each tree telling you when the time is right. As outdoor bonsai mature, the bark develops fissures and the soil becomes covered in moss. Outdoor bonsai bring you closer to nature and introduce greater challenges and more possibilities, which is why they are preferred by the connoisseur.

Almost all hardy bonsai are produced in Japan. Generally, they are field-grown for between five and twenty years, sometimes even longer, but nowadays rarely collected from the wild; those that are tend to remain in Japan. While in the open ground, the trees receive some pruning and shaping before being lifted and examined. The trees

Right: Thousands of *Acer palmatum* starter trees under protection in a Japanese nursery

Below: Driftwood-style bonsai created from wild plants collected from the mountains. These are becoming increasingly rare and are now very expensive

with the most potential or with the fewest imperfections are retained for further development and the rest are exported as cheap 'starter' trees.

The cycle is repeated, and each time the best are retained and the rest are exported at an appropriately higher price than the last batch. And at each successive cycle the standard of workmanship and the time taken over aesthetic consideration is increased. The essence of Japanese bonsai is the quest for perfection and this system serves to maximize the artistic as well as the commercial potential of each particular tree.

Buying a bonsai

Bonsai are traditionally expensive, largely because they have to travel half way round the world to reach you. Because of the high cost, you should understand what you are buying, and make sure you get the best deal.

Buying a bonsai

Your first introduction to bonsai might well have been when you received one as a gift. If so, you're not alone. Almost half of all the imported tropical and sub-tropical bonsai are bought as gifts. On the other hand, you may have seen bonsai on display and decided you want to try keeping your own. Either way, the fact that you are reading this book indicates that you are interested enough to learn more, and to acquire more bonsai.

High Street bonsai

Bonsai have a reputation of being expensive which, as we saw in Chapter One, is often true. But you may not always get what you think you are paying for. Just before Christmas, so-called 'bonsai' crop up everywhere – street markets, garage forecourts, even car boot sales and flea markets, and you should beware of all of these. Some such traders will, no doubt, offer good quality products at a reasonable price, but they are a minority. Shop around and compare prices and general health. Bear in mind that prices will fall in the January sales.

Japanese bonsai properly displayed in a nursery, each tree receiving adequate light and air to keep it healthy

Department stores also stock up with a number of indoor bonsai just before the Christmas rush. The better ones will offer trees recently imported from the far east. They will have spent weeks in a dark container, then in a heated greenhouse before winding up on the shelf. Most will be tough enough to recover if properly cared for but generally in-store care is poor. Stores with a keener eye for an easy buck might offer minute recently rooted cuttings, in shallow pots, packed in carton boxes with a clear window. This keeps the plant green for a while, but the lack of light and fresh air weakens it tremendously. It is best not to buy

these at all. If you do, you will be paying for the packaging which, if the plant is to survive, must be discarded immediately.

Mail order

Many specialist nurseries offer a mail-order service. They pack the trees well and generally use contract carriers for next-day delivery. If you are unable to get to a specialist nursery and you are happy buying a bonsai without seeing it, then mail order is worth a try. Check first whether or not the supplier offers a refund for trees damaged on arrival, and unpack the tree while the delivery man is still at the door.

Advertisements in consumer magazines for mail-order bonsai should always be regarded with the utmost suspicion.

Specialist nurseries

There is no doubt that specialist nurseries are far and away the best places to buy bonsai. They depend on year-round business and rely heavily on repeat customers, so they have to be good. Most are run by people who became hooked on bonsai and turned their hobby into a business. As such, they have a good knowledge of bonsai care which they are always happy to pass on. They also stock all the bonsai paraphernalia such as training wire, tools, pots, fertilisers and so on. Many will offer holiday care and 'hospital' facilities for sick trees. They may also offer a repotting and pruning service, but after reading this book you shouldn't need either!

Wherever you decide to buy your bonsai, you should first arm yourself with a little knowledge to enable you to choose a good buy.

Health

Bonsai spend weeks in a shipping container and six months in quarantine before being offered for sale. By the time they reach the sales benches they should be in perfect condition. But, unlike plants in garden nurseries, bonsai can spend many months, or even years, waiting to be bought. With the best will in the world, some will inevitably contract various ailments or suffer from an unintentional lack of attention from time to time. Always check trees from the bottom upward.

Gently try to rock the trunk to see if the tree is secure in its pot. If it rocks easily the roots are not completely filling the pot for some reason. This may mean that they are rotting or, at least, not growing well. Check that the drainage holes are adequate and are not blocked with roots. The presence of moss on the soil is a good sign, but water-loving plants like liverwort indicate poor soil conditions.

• Look for old wounds which were not sealed properly and may be decaying. This can be difficult to arrest and may eventually cause more serious problems.

• Dead shoots may be a normal reaction to the lack of light and air caused by congested foliage. In these

Tropical bonsai need to be kept in an artificial environment – in the nursery and in the home. At this nursery the conditions are ideal for the health and vigour of the plants

cases there is absolutely nothing to worry about because the shoots will readily regenerate once the tree receives your attention. Dead branches, though, are another matter. The loss of a branch may be caused by wire constriction, disease, root ailments or mistreatment.

• Yellowing leaves can mean over-or under-watering, insufficient light or a deficiency of trace elements, particularly magnesium. All these are easily cured, but that should be the nursery's responsibility not yours. Yellow leaves may also indicate more serious root problems so try the trunk-rocking test.

• Dry areas of foliage can be caused by temporary conditions such as draught or drought. This may also be caused by infestations of spider mites. In either case, if the leaves have totally withered, the likelihood is that the shoots have done likewise, perhaps even the entire branch.

• Finally, check the foliage for pests and evidence of fungal disease. Distorted or discoloured leaves are normally caused by one or the other. Fortunately, most are easily cured but, once again, this should be the nursery's job.

Shape

The most important thing is that you find the shape of your bonsai pleasing, but don't be fooled by a dense canopy of bright green leaves. Trees have an internal structure of trunk and branches that also needs to be examined. The standard of workmanship that has gone into shaping the tree will also affect its quality. As with the health check, start at the bottom.

• On outdoor bonsai, the roots should be evenly distributed around the trunk and should flair naturally as they enter the soil. Twisted, crossing or uneven visible roots are particularly ugly and generally impossible to rectify. On indoor trees, which follow the Chinese style, the roots are normally intentionally exposed and randomly arranged. Here the emphasis is on the bizarre, but they should still appear natural.

• Many desirable varieties are grafted onto root stocks of a similar variety. Graft unions almost always leave a permanent scar and often swell, disfiguring the trunk. Poor graft unions get worse as time passes, not better. Japanese white pine (*Pinus parviflora*) are always grafted onto black pine (*Pinus thunbergii*) root stocks. The union is made just below the first branch to take advantage of the black

Above: Beware of poor grafts, especially on maples. The swelling will get worse as time passes

Left: A tangled root mass like this is inefficient and will require reorganising if the plant is to progress

pine's fissured bark. Normally the first branch is trained to hide the graft union, so make sure this branch is healthy and does its job properly.

• Trunks have an infinite variety of shapes – on indoor trees they may be coiled or dramatically bent back on themselves. On outdoor trees they are more likely to follow conventional tree-like forms. In either case, the trunk should taper from base to apex and should be clear of branches for about the bottom third. It should also be completely free of ugly scars. With group or forest plantings, the trunks should be varied in height, thickness and spacing, and no one trunk should obscure another.

• Mass-produced bonsai are wire-trained just like any other, and are often exported with the wire still on. This is not a problem in itself, but it is not uncommon to find that the wire has already begun to cut into the bark, causing spiral scars that will take many years to heal. Occasionally you may find bonsai with wire deeply embedded in the bark and impossible to remove. Don't believe the myth that this is done to artificially 'age' the tree. It is the result of carelessness and nothing else.

• All bonsai are hard pruned at some point in their preparation for sale, and all pruning will leave a scar of some sort. When working on your own trees, carefully hollow out the wound and seal it *(see Chapter Seven)*. However, this is not practical on a commercial scale, so short stubs are left which can be cut off and hollowed out when you get the tree home. Before you buy, consider how this could be done. A trunk that has been cut through at right angles to reduce height and induce branching will not only have an unnatural shape, but the large scar will be a permanent feature. A good bonsai should either show no scars at all or should have all pruning wounds incorporated into the design, by carving them into natural-looking hollows or shaping and bleaching the stubs to create jins (*see Chapter Seven*).

• The easiest way to learn how to assess the branch structure of a bonsai is to look at the full-size trees around you. On old conifers the branches are horizontal or sweep downward and each bears wide shallow pads of foliage. The branches become progressively shorter and thinner as they become higher up the trunk, giving the tree a conical shape. On deciduous trees branches are horizontal or sweep gently upward, frequently forking. Each branch bears a mass of foliage which forms part of the overall dome-shaped canopy. Branches are distributed evenly around the trunk. Making allowances for scale and the desire for an 'interesting' shape, the same principle applies to bonsai, albeit in a simpli-

Right: Wire scars on branches or trunks weakens the tree and will take many years to heal

Below: Trident maples readily form a strong buttress at the base of the trunk, much prized in Japan

fied way. Check for wire marks and ugly pruning scars. Also, avoid trees with two branches positioned immediately opposite each other. These 'bar branches' will jar the eye

and in the future will cause the trunk to swell where they join it.

Species

Before buying a bonsai you must consider where it will be expected to live. If you want a tree for indoors, assess the light and temperature levels in the room, and decide whether or not you can put the tree outside during summer. If you prefer outdoor bonsai, you need to consider the amount of sunlight your garden receives. Can you provide dappled shade all day or protection from the hot afternoon sun? The following pages provide a guide to the species which are suitable for various domestic environments.

Bright sunny rooms

Many modern homes have large picture-windows which allow in plenty of light. South or west-facing windows will also admit hot sun whose effect is amplified by the glass. Many species will suffer in these conditions, and should be kept away from the direct sun, but close enough to the window to receive good light. Don't keep your trees on the windowsill because at night the temperature close to the glass can fall dramatically, particularly in winter when the central heating is off. This constant extreme temperature fluctuation can be fatal to tropical and sub-tropical bonsai. Positioning trees some distance from the window will reduce the strength of the sunlight and broaden the range of species you can successfully grow.

Right: Podocarpus love bright, warm conditions and will thrive close to a large sunny window in a centrally heated flat

Suitable species
- Bamboos
- Bougainvillea
- Lagerstroemia
- Ligustrum
- Murraya
- Olive
- *Punica granatum*
- Pistachio
- Podocarpus
- Serrissa
- *Ulmus parvifolia*

parts receive adequate light. The lights generate slight heat which can also benefit the trees, but the drying effect of this needs to be countered by regular spraying and extra vigilance when watering.

Suitable species
- Carmona
- Cycas
- Ficus
- Myrtus
- Nandina
- Sageretia

Dull rooms

North or east-facing rooms may appear quite dull but close to the window there will be sufficient light to keep several species perfectly happy.

One solution to the problem of low natural light is to install purpose-built artificial lighting for your bonsai collection. This is not as costly or impractical as it might at first seem. Although there are a number of horticultural lighting systems on the market, ordinary, blue-white fluorescent strip lighting provides the complete spectrum of light needed by most species, and is cheap to run. The drawback is that their light is fairly low intensity. Ideally, the strips should be positioned between 200 and 300mm (8 and 12 in) from the foliage. Use three strips, positioning two directly above the trees – one toward the front and another further back – and the third lower down, behind the trees. Keep the lights on for seven to ten hours a day and rotate the trees through 90 degrees every few days to ensure all

Above right: Extra light can be provided by placing two or three fluorescent strip lights directly above the trees

Right: Ficus are tough plants that are accustomed to the shadier, more humid conditions below taller trees

Sunny gardens

In mid-summer, the heat from the after-noon sun is reflected off fences, buildings and patios, sending the local temperature soaring. Pots heat up and dry out rapidly. The sunlight is intense and can itself be damaging, particularly in recent years, when its harmful rays are not so efficiently filtered by the atmosphere. Some species, especially when grown in pots, dislike such intense, hot sun – others positively love it. But all bonsai should have their pots shaded or regularly cooled with water during very hot spells in order to prevent the roots from becoming too hot and cooking. Erecting a purpose-built shaded area will enable you to grow a wider range of species.

Right: Chinese juniper are adapted to life on exposed mountains where they receive full sun. Providing similar conditions in your garden will keep the foliage compact

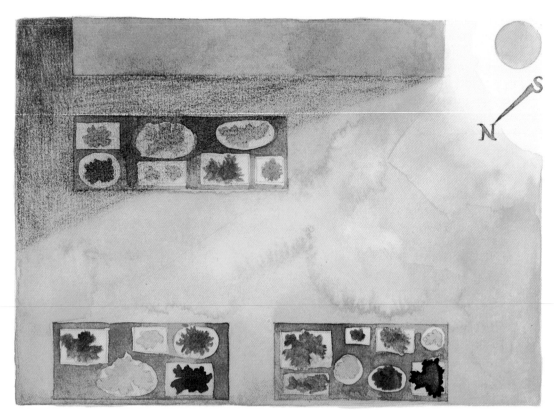

Suitable species
• Celtis
• Chaenomeles
• Chinese juniper
• Cotoneaster
• Cryptomeria
• *Ilex crenata*
• Needle juniper
• Malus
• Picea
• White pine
• Black pine
• Pyracantha
• Ulmus
• Wisteria

Shaded gardens

In many ways a shaded garden provides the ideal environment for bonsai, provided the sky directly above your bonsai is not obscured by overhanging trees and the sun is reflected off a wall or fence into the garden for at least part of the day to maintain seasonal temperatures. Even species that prefer full sun will do quite nicely with good overhead light, although the growth might be a little 'leggy'. This can be controlled by reducing the nitrogen in the feeding programme and regular trimming.

Right: The foliage, flowers and coloured bark of Stewartia all perform best in shadier conditions

Suitable species
- Azaleas
- Japanese maples
- Trident maple
- Hornbeams
- Ginkgo
- Yew
- Chamaecyparis
- Beech
- Stewartia
- Zelkova

How a tree works

It is easy enough to carry out the instructions that follow regarding watering, feeding and pruning, but understanding a little about how a tree functions will increase your enjoyment of bonsai and give you more confidence in caring for your trees.

Roots

Because the roots are out of sight, it is very easy to overlook the importance of a healthy, vigorous root system. More often than not, when a bonsai begins to look sickly it is an indication of some form of root disorder.

Roots have three functions. First, they provide anchorage, holding the tree firm in the ground. In the wild they do this by growing in all directions and eventually thicken to form a buttress at the base of the trunk. Second, they absorb moisture and soluble nutrients from the soil. Third, they store sugars during dormancy, to provide energy for the first flush of growth in spring. Let's look at these functions in more detail.

Anchorage

This may seem rather irrelevant to bonsai but in fact the roots are still responsible for holding the tree firm in the pot. You will see in the section on repotting (see page 48) that wire can be used to hold the tree firm initially, but this is unsightly and is therefore only temporary. If the roots lack vigour or are decaying, they will not fill the pot and the trunk will rock in the wind or as you work on the tree. This causes further damage to the roots, and so the vicious circle continues.

Left: The plump, white growing tips indicate a healthy and vigorous root system

To hold a tree firm in its pot, the roots must be distributed all around the trunk and must grow sideways rather than downward. One-sided root systems are unstable and will most likely also result in a one-sided branch structure. Roots that grow steeply downward before spreading sideways tend to rely more on fine roots to provide anchorage.

Absorbing water and nutrients

Healthy, growing roots show plump and white at the tips. This is the most active part of the root system. The very tip is protected as it thrusts its way through the soil by a hard cap which is constantly being worn away and replaced. Behind this, the white part of the root is clothed in minute root hairs, which are composed of a single cell and can be almost invisible to the naked eye. Although water can be absorbed by older parts of the root, it is through these root hairs that the water and, most importantly, nutrients are more readily absorbed due to their enormous com-

bined surface area. Root hair production is stimulated by moisture and oxygen present in the soil.

Absorption of water takes place by the process of osmosis. The membranes surrounding root cells are semi-permeable – which means they have millions of tiny pores just big enough to allow one water molecule to pass through. When the concentration of nutrient salts inside the root is greater than immediately outside, water molecules pass through the pores, into the root hairs to dilute the solution. This means that the solution of salts in the root hairs is now weaker than in the adjacent cell, so water molecules pass one cell further into the root, and so on. Once the water has reached the xylem cells in the core of

scopic process takes place hundreds of millions of times a day.

the root it is drawn up the tree by capillary action.

The pores in the semi-permeable membrane are big enough to allow water molecules to pass, but not dissolved nutrients. They are absorbed electrochemically. All the chemicals in question are either positively or negatively charged. When the tree requires a particular nutrient – say, potash – which is positively charged, the root expels a positively charged hydrogen ion to make way for it. Simultaneously, one pore changes size and shape to allow just one potassium ion through into the root.

Nobody is sure how the tree can judge its nutrient requirements so precisely, but this remarkable micro-

Root burn
If the concentration of salts outside the roots is greater than that inside, the osmosis is reversed and water passes out of the roots back into the soil to equalize the solutions. The tree will wilt and begin to shed young shoots. This is why you should never use fertilisers in excess of the recommended rates or when the roots are inactive. Similarly, feeding directly after repotting, when there are few, if any, root hairs, can have a similar effect. Regular pro-longed watering to flush the soil clean of residual salts is a wise precaution.

Nutrient storage
Older, thicker roots develop bundles of sap-conducting cells called the phloem, which is also present in the trunk and branches. These cells conduct the sugars from the leaves and distribute them to all parts of the plant,

Above: The spreading roots on this azalea look like fingers, grasping the soil. This type of root structure is efficient as well as imparting strength and character to the tree

wherever they are needed for growth, including to the roots. In late summer and autumn, when growth slows down and eventually ceases, the phloem be-comes plump with excess sugars which are stored there until they are needed to support new growth in spring. Transplanting trees and pruning roots in autumn causes consider-able loss of stored sugars which will retard spring growth. This is why you should wait until the buds begin to swell, which indi-cates that at least some of

the stored sugars have been returned to the grow-ing points, before pruning the roots. The exceptions are some flowering plants which seem to produce even more flowers and fruit if given a hard time and repotted in autumn.

Trunks and branches

The main purpose of the trunk and branches of a tree is purely structural, i.e., to support as much foliage as possible in positions where it will receive the most light and air. They also, naturally, have to conduct water, nutrients and sugars from roots to leaves and back. In a mature tree most of the tissue forming the trunk and branches – the heartwood – is dead. It has become lignified (literally, turned into wood) and hardened, and is responsible for the tree's strength. Naturally, the thicker the heartwood, the more difficult it is to bend. The actual living part of the trunk and branches is confined to the outermost layers, and it is here that all the activity takes place .

The cambium

If you gently scratch a twig with your fingernail you will notice a bright green layer just below the surface. This is the cambium, a single layer of cells surrounding the trunk, branches and shoots. The cambium is constantly developing new cells of different types both on the inside and the outside, throughout the growing season. It also has the ability to initiate new buds or new roots, and to fuse with the cambium of another plant, such as when grafting.

When a thick branch is cut through during the growing season the cambium has a heyday. It responds to the loss of a branch by generating a mass of completely new shoots which emerge like a crown from between the bark and the sapwood in an attempt to replace the lost foliage. Most of these shoots will die off through overcrowding and lack of light, but the strongest will continue to grow vigorously.

The cambium is also responsible for producing the healing tissue that rolls over wounds. If you look closely at a recent pruning cut, you can see how this tissue emerges from between the bark and the wood.

The xylem

On the inside of the cambium the new cells it produces form the xylem, which conducts the water upward. It is the formation of new xylem each year that creates the familiar annual rings. The xylem remains active for a year or more, depending on the species and while active, forms what is referred to as sapwood. This is the lighter coloured group of rings surrounding the heartwood. The rate of a tree's growth and the pattern of its xylem cells determine the strength and grain of its wood.

The production of new xylem is also what makes branches set in position when trained with wire. Once the tensile strength of the new xylem is sufficient to counter that of the old wood, the wire may be removed and the branch will stay in place. The wood in young shoots and

Above: Deciduous trees such as maples reward you with year-round interest as they change in response to the seasons

Right: The broad, spreading foliage pads of this Cedar of Lebanon are typical of ancient conifers and provide inspiration for the bonsai artist

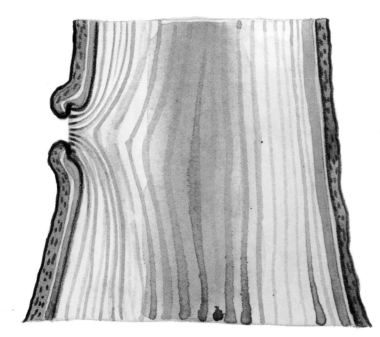

branchlets is composed entirely of xylem which is malleable and will readily adopt new shapes. Older branches that contain heartwood take longer to set. The tensions created by bending the branch will always be present, and even if a branch appears to have set, it may well gradually move back toward its original position as the soft xylem yields under pressure from the tough heartwood.

The phloem

On the outside of the cambium the new cells form the phloem, which distributes the sugars manufactured by the leaves to all other parts of the plant. As old phloem cells are replaced by new ones each year, they in turn harden and become the bark. As the years pass the bark thickens and in most cases becomes corky and flakes, peels or develops fissures. The precise formation of phloem cells and the length of their useful lives differs between one species and another. This explains why different trees display their own unique characteristic bark patterns as they mature.

Why bonsai live so long

In the wild, a healthy tree will continue growing until it reaches its genetically pre-determined

Above: Each year a new layer of wood is formed which gradually 'rolls' over wounds until they are completely healed

Above right: When thick branches are pruned, masses of new shoots emerge from the cambium layer, between the bark and the sapwood. Most of these will die off through overcrowding and only the strongest will continue to grow

height. Once this has been achieved the crown begins to spread sideways, generally forming a dome. Eventually, the distance between the active roots at the periphery of the root system and the increasing mass of foliage at the tips of the branches become too great and the tree begins to deteriorate. As the foliage receives less water and nutrients from the roots it is therefore less able to supply adequate sugars to generate new roots and the tree eventually dies.

Trees that are regularly pruned, such as those that are pollarded or hedgerow trees, live for much longer than their full-size counterparts because they never

reach their maximum dimensions. They will not die of old age until the structural heartwood rots and collapses.

Because a bonsai is constantly being encouraged, by pruning, to produce new healthy roots and shoots, it is always actively growing, trying to reach maturity. The actual living part – the cambium, flanked by the xylem and the phloem – is never more than a few years old. Provided enough growth takes place each year to lay down sufficient new xylem and phloem to sustain the tree, a bonsai will always remain essentially young and should, in theory at least, live for ever.

Leaves

Each leaf is a highly efficient food factory that converts water from the soil and carbon dioxide from the air into essential sugars in a process called photosynthesis. As this term implies, light – normally sunlight – is an important catalyst in this process. Without sufficient light the leaves lose much of their green chlorophyll, the substance that enables photosynthesis to take place, consequently losing their ability to function.

Some shade is preferable for almost all plants grown in containers, but deep shade will cause problems, as will excessive sun. Too much sun, although providing the necessary light, will cause the leaves to overheat. They will rapidly close their breathing pores (stomata) in order to reduce water evaporation. This effectively causes the leaf to 'shut down' until the sun becomes less intense. During this time the leaf is not manufacturing sugars because the process relies on a constant passage of water through the leaf and also a constant supply of carbon dioxide which is absorbed through the same stomata. Precisely how much sun is too much depends entirely on the species.

Leaf types

Plants that normally live in semi shade, such as azaleas and Japanese maples, have delicate, thin-skinned leaves which will easily become brown and withered at the edges if grown in full sun or if exposed to drying winds. At the other end of the scale, plants which normally live exposed to the hot sun have thick, leathery leaves, often with a waxy coating which helps prevent water evaporation. A similar waxy coating is also used by some species that prefer extremely cold conditions. Most conifers have waxy leaves, but this time the idea is essentially to protect them from the cold, and also to help prevent snow and frost from adhering to the needles.

The variety of leaf colour and shape is endless. This variety is what makes collecting different species so fascinating. The size can also vary considerably, not only between species, but also even within the same variety, depending on the growing conditions of the individual plant. Plants growing in the ground or in large containers in semi-shade will bear large, deep green leaves. The same variety growing in a small bonsai pot in full sun will have much smaller leaves which will not display the same richness of colour.

A waxy coating conserves water and protects against freezing

Following stress, the foliage becomes more open for a season or two

Above: No waxy coating is necessary
Below: A thick waxy coating protects against severe cold or hot sun

Buds

On most species there is a tiny, embryonic bud at the base of each leaf stalk (petiole). Take a cabbage and slice it in half and you will see a greatly magnified version of a typical bud – for that is what a cabbage is. You will also be able to see the smaller buds at the bases of the petioles. As the bud opens in spring, the central core elongates to form at the shoot with leaves distributed at intervals (internodes) along its length. As it extends the bud at the growing tip is constantly undergoing a cycle of opening, extension and regeneration. If this is removed the energy will be diverted into the next one or two buds back down the shoot.

Each bud is surrounded by scales which can be anything from green, through browns to bright red, depending on the species. The scales are designed to protect the delicate partly formed leaves in the bud from the sun, rain, frost and insect attack. They are, in fact, modified leaves and, as such, also have embryonic buds at the base of each scale. This explains why a mass of new shoots emerge from the short stub left when hard pruning current year's growth.

Buds can also be formed on old wood in reaction to more severe pruning or to some other trauma. The cambium layer works to regenerate lost foliage by rapidly developing new buds which force their way through the bark. These are called adventitious buds and can appear on branches, trunks and even on old roots near the surface of the soil. When you see a tree in the countryside that has lots of adventitious buds on its trunk and branches, you can be sure that it has recently suffered some kind of trauma – either drought, physical damage or perhaps a severe attack of some fungal disease or insect pest. In bonsai cultivation the production of adventitious buds is of key importance because they are selectively used to grow new shoots to replace outgrown or congested areas of foliage.

Buds are a useful indicator of the state of a tree's growth in spring. As the tree begins to stir from its dormancy, the buds start to swell. Tiny paler coloured lines will be seen at the edge of each scale as they begin to separate. This indicates an increase in root activity and tells us to get on with the repotting before growth is too far advanced.

Autumn colour

One of the most charming and rewarding aspects of trees, large or small, is the vivid autumn coloration which can vary from bright yellow through reds to purple. Many of these coloured pigments are in the leaves from the time the shoots emerge from the buds but are masked by the presence of chlorophyll. In red-leaved maples the pigments exist in greater quantity than the chlorophyll, so the masking effect is reversed. Grow a red-leaved maple in deep shade and it will produce more chlorophyll and turn green. If kept in a brighter position the leaves may stay red all summer. Other pigments are the result of chemical changes that take place in early autumn. As autumn approaches the leaves cease producing sugars and the chlorophyll breaks down and, along with other minerals, is re-absorbed by the plant.

Autumn colour can be enhanced by keeping your trees in a warm sunny spot during the day in late summer and early autumn, but keeping them as cold as possible at night. This ensures that the colour-forming breakdown of substances continues at maximum rate during the day but their redistribution to other parts of the plant is hindered by the night-time cold.

Don't worry if your bonsai lose their leaves before full-sized trees lose theirs. This is quite common and, although disappointing, does no harm.

Right: This magnified bud reveals a tightly-compressed mass of embryonic leaves, complete with stem and another terminal bud

Below: The upper surface of a leaf absorbs sunlight which helps convert water and carbon dioxide into nourishing sugars. The underside contains the pores – stomata – through which the plant breathes

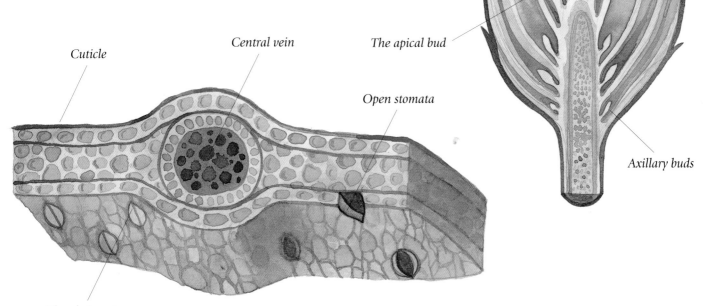

Cuticle

Central vein

Open stomata

Closed stomata

Bud scales

The apical bud

Axillary buds

Light, water and air

All plants need an adequate supply of light, water and air but there is a world of difference between sunlight and sunshine, between moist and waterlogged soil or between fresh air and a draught.

Left: Delicate leaves, such as those on Japanese maples, are easily scorched if exposed to drying winds

or juniper, when kept close to a wall, will grow vigorously on the open side but may even start to die back on the shaded side.

On the other hand, if you keep a maple or an azalea, both plants of woodland margins and valleys, in an exposed situation, the side away from the sun will produce much healthier and more vigorous growth. The leaves of red maples will hold their colour for longer if kept in semi-shade although returning them to full sun in autumn will greatly intensify seasonal colour.

In bonsai we try to strike a happy medium. Few people can provide perfect conditions for all species, but most can find a sunny corner or erect some shade netting. Your bonsai isn't going to die through too much or too little sunlight – but it will tell you that it's not happy.

One final point. Remember to turn each bonsai through 90 degrees every few days, so that each area of foliage receives an equal amount of light.

Water

Surprisingly, more bonsai – or any other type of pot plant – are lost through overwatering than through drought. Very few species can tolerate permanently

Light

As we saw in Chapter Three, leaves need a certain amount of sunlight in order to photosynthesize and nourish the plant with sugars. In too shady conditions leaves will grow larger to gather as much light as possible, the internodes (distances between leaves) will increase as the plant rapidly tries to extend shoots to reach through the overhead canopy to the sun. In good light, leaves will be smaller and internodes much shorter. If the sun is too strong, many

plants will throw out new growth from close to the trunk, where they are shaded by the scorched outer foliage. Many plants also use day length, rather than temperature, to trigger seasonal phases such as flowering or leaf-fall.

Bearing in mind, of course, that different species prefer different amounts of sunlight, it is important to learn a little about the natural habitat of the full-size cousins of your bonsai. Pines and junipers that are found growing on exposed mountain sides are naturally adapted to tolerate full sun. Indeed, growth can be rather disappointing when grown in shady conditions. A bonsai pine

Right: Insufficient light causes the shoots to become leggy and the internodes (spaces between the leaves) to extend out of proportion to the tree

Left: Coloured foliage can become green if light levels are too low. The upper leaves here remain red while those they are shading are beginning to turn green

Some species – known as calcifuges – do not tolerate lime, which may cause problems in areas where the tapwater is 'hard', or rich in lime. Using an acid, organic-based soil and giving regular applications of a proprietary soil-acidifier will counteract hard water. In extreme cases, exposed roots may become encrusted with lime deposit, which is harmless but unsightly. This can be removed with a stiff toothbrush. Never use artificially 'softened' water. Water softeners replace the calcium with sodium, which is even worse.

Tapwater contains all manner of added chemicals which are designed to 'purify' it, or to strengthen our teeth and so on. None of these chemicals are particularly harmful to plants in low concentrations. However, occasionally higher than normal quantities of chlorine are introduced, particularly when water supplies are low or are drawn from rivers, and the weather is warm. If you allow the water to stand in an open container for a few hours before use the chlorine will evaporate.

Allowing the water to stand also brings it to the ambient temperature. Applying ice-cold water to a sun-warmed pot can shock the root system and cause temporary damage

saturated soil and some prefer dry roots for part of the year (*for details of these see the Tree Directory*). But most require soil that remains moist at the driest and is never allowed to dry out completely between waterings.

If you are not sure whether your trees need watering, gently scratch away the surface of the soil to see how damp it is underneath. If it is just damp, then you can apply water, if it is wet, then leave it alone. If the soil is bone dry, water immediately using the immersion technique described below. After a while, you should be able to judge how wet the soil is simply by the weight of the pot.

Water quality

Without doubt, rainwater is by far the best for all plants, even in these days of acid rain. However, it is not always possible to collect sufficient rainwater to last more than a week or so in high summer. Storing large quantities of water for a long time has its dangers too. Air-borne spores of fungi such as phytopthera can enter the tank and, when watered into the pot, will attack the roots of your bonsai. Always keep water barrels tightly closed, and flush them out with disinfectant and clean tap water at regular intervals.

Right: Poorly drained soil will rapidly compact and become waterlogged. In soil like this the roots cannot breathe and will soon begin to rot

to the delicate growing tips. On the other hand, water that is a few degrees cooler than the roots will refresh them and cool them down on hot days. The trick is to water either in the early morning or in the evening, when the roots are not so overheated. If you have a large collection of bonsai, you may choose to use a hose with a fine spray attachment for watering. Remember: if a hose is left lying in the sun all day the water in it will become very hot indeed. Always let the water run for a few minutes before using it on your trees.

Overhead watering

Obviously, the most natural way for a plant to receive water is from above. If your bonsai are properly potted – with the free-draining soil level just below the rim of the pot – this method should never cause a problem. However, there are a few points to watch.

• Use a fine rose spray attachment to your hose or watering can. Excessive force will wash away the surface soil and tend to compact the rest.

• Fill the space between the surface of the soil and the rim of the pot with water and allow it to completely soak in. Then repeat the process. By this time water should be emerging from the drainage holes in the pot.

• If no water emerges from the drainage holes after two applications it might mean that the soil is too compact or in poor condition, or perhaps the drainage holes are blocked. Unblock the drainage holes and, in future, use the immersion watering technique described below until you repot the tree at the earliest appropriate time.

• Make sure you water the whole of the surface of the soil. The area behind the trunk is frequently neglected when watering in a hurry, and this can weaken the roots in that area as well as the branches directly above them.

• Avoid the temptation to give all your bonsai the same amount of water every day. Watering *en masse* is all right for a limited period in summer, but check the pots individually every few days and adjust the watering as necessary.

• Don't water in full sun unless the water has been allowed to stand for an hour or two.

• The leaves will enjoy being wetted at watering time provided that they are not in full sun at the time. If you are using foliar feeds, or if the water is particularly hard, powdery

Below: Immersion watering. Immersing the entire pot in water every so often drives out all the stale air and ensures that there are no persistent dry spots. When the bubbles stop rising the pot can be removed from the water and drained

deposits may appear on the foliage. This will normally wash off when it next rains.

Immersion watering

When bonsai trees are potbound the roots become so dense that water is very slow to penetrate. You may see water running from the drainage holes but this may have merely trickled between the soil and the pot, without wetting the soil at all.

Imported indoor bonsai are generally planted in dense clay-like soils which may be fine in the growing nursery but are not appropriate for long-term use in domestic conditions. The soil becomes very compacted and is reluctant to absorb water. Furthermore, the soil is frequently mounded up above the rim of the pot so that the water just runs off before it has had a chance to soak in. In conditions like these the immersion technique can get you and your bonsai out of trouble.

The immersion technique for watering bonsai: place the bonsai in a bowl or bath and slowly add water until it covers the surface of the soil entirely. You should see bubbles rising from the soil as the water replaces the air in the soil. If no bubbles

appear it may be because the soil is very compacted. Wait until the bubbles have stopped rising (or for half an hour if there were no bubbles) and then remove the pot from the water. Tilt the pot to drain off excess water. A number of enthusiasts who normally water from overhead immerse all their pots once a month to ensure there are no hidden areas of dry roots.

Automatic watering

Many commercial plant nurseries use a variety of automatic watering systems ranging from overhead sprays to individual drip-feeds. These are fine if you want to maintain a large number of virtually identical plants, but not so reliable when each plant requires more individual attention. Some experienced bonsai growers use timed low level sprays or drip feeds while they are away from home, but they need extremely careful planning. The best advice is not to use automatic systems at all.

Air

Like people, trees need fresh air in order to remain healthy. Poor air circulation, either around the leaves and branches or around the roots (see page 48), will result in poor, sickly growth and creates ideal conditions for fungal and bacterial spores to take hold. Indoor bonsai that spend their lives in centrally heated, smoke-filled rooms will suffer just as badly as humans. The only difference is that the effect will be much more pronounced. Inner shoots will wither, leaves will become covered in powdery mildew, insects will colonize the foliage and the soil and trunk will become covered in algae.

To maintain good air circulation, indoors or outdoors, bonsai should be placed at about waist-height, preferably on their own stand indoors or on slatted benches outside.

Right: Yellowing leaves may seem to be caused by dry soil but, more often than not, they result from overwatering or draughts

Below: Automatic watering systems ensure an even amount of water is supplied to every plant, but they take no account of each plant's individual needs

This allows air of ambient temperature to circulate freely around all parts of the tree. Indoors, If placed lower the air will be cooler than room temperature; if placed higher it will be warmer – and drier. Outdoors, trees that are placed too low will not only be short-changed as far as fresh air is concerned, but they will also be prey to all the neighbourhood snails, slugs and, worst of all, cats!

However, it is important to recognize the difference between fresh air circulation and draughts. A draught is a fast-moving current, usually colder than the surrounding air. Its effect can be devastating, causing rapid yellowing and shedding of leaves and die-back of young shoots. The pot cools down rapidly, restricting root growth. Once you have found a situation that seems to suit your bonsai, leave it there.

Outdoors, wind can also be harmful to bonsai. Clearly, strong winds can tear at the foliage of any species which not only disfigures the leaves but also reduces their efficiency. Even moderate winds can have a severe drying effect which is as dangerous during winter as it is in summer. Species that are adapted to live in the relative protection of woodland margins or sheltered valleys, such as azaleas, Japanese maples and hornbeams, will develop brown edges to the leaves if exposed to wind.

Half-hardy see Hardy.

Hardening-off The process of gradually introducing a plant which has been grown in sheltered or protected conditions to the rigours of the outside environment. This is done by allowing it to stay outside in the open during the day, or in mild spells, and returning the plant to its protection at night.

Hardy Describes a plant which is able to survive outside during the winter.

Hokidachi The bonsai style known as broom or besom. This is probably the most 'tree-like' of all bonsai styles and consists of a number of branches all issuing from the same point at the top of an upright trunk. These branches divide and sub-divide regularly until they form a fine tracery of twigs.

Hybrid The offspring of parents of different species, or different forms of a species.

Ikadabuki Raft-style bonsai. This style is created by laying a tree on its side and training all the conveniently placed branches upwards. All the branches which point downwards or which are not suitably sited are removed. The original trunk is then buried in the soil and eventually produces roots along its length. The new trunks are then trained in the normal way into any suitable style. Eventually it will be possible to remove all the original root ball, allowing the tree to be supported by the new roots. This is an ideal method for producing group plantings since there is no competition between individual plants.

Inflorescence The flowerbearing part of a plant.

Internode The distance between the leaf nodes on a shoot. It is this distance which dictates whether or not a particular plant has the growth characteristics suitable for bonsai culture.

Jin The most commonly used Japanese term in bonsai culture and one of the most difficult to define concisely. A jin is a branch or the apex of a tree which has had its bark removed and has been treated with a preservation bleach such as lime sulphur in order to simulate the naturally occurring dead sunbleached branches commonly found on old pines and junipers. The judicious use of jins can have a great effect on the aesthetics of a bonsai by counterbalancing areas of foliage where another area of foliage would be considered too heavy. A terminal or apecal jin can also be used to create the illusion of a fine tip to a tree where this effect would, for one reason or another be impossible to achieve with foliage. The appearance of great age and a lifetimes struggle against the elements can be bestowed on a bonsai by the use of jins, which may also be carved and shaped into abstract sculptural forms.

Jukei The Japanese word for 'style', describing the shape or form of a bonsai.

Kabudachi Clump-style bonsai, where all the trunks emanate from closely located points on the same root. This style is often created by cutting a trunk down to ground level and allowing several new trunks to grow from around the cut. In full-sized trees this process is known as coppicing.

Kengai Cascade-style bonsai. To qualify as a true cascade the lowest point of the tree must be below the bottom of its container.

Korabuki Multi-trunked style of bonsai.

Kyuhon-yose A nine-trunked bonsai.

Kyonal A proprietary Japanese product used for dressing wounds after pruning. It has a plasticine-like consistency but never dries out or goes hard. This means that as the wound heals the kyonal is forced out and does not become enveloped by the new growth. It is easy to use, and coloured so as to conceal the wound and blend with the bark.

Layering A means of propagation from woody shoots or branches involving the removal of a band of bark around the chosen shoot about one and half times the thickness of the shoot. The shoot is then either pegged to the ground and covered with soil or wrapped with damp sphagnum moss and enclosed in polythene. After a time roots should appear, and once they have established the shoot can be severed from the parent and potted up.

Leaching The process by which nutrients and other soluble minerals are removed from the soil by water draining through. To counteract this phenomenon bonsai growers recommend applying more regular (but weaker) feeds.

Leader The main, vertical stem or shoot of a young plant. The dominant shoot which extends fastest and dictates the directional thrust of the tree's growth. Also used to describe the dominant shoot on a branch or smaller twig.

Leaf mould Partially decayed dead leaves which have broken down to a crumbly texture and which should be used as a substitute for peat. Deciduous leaves, especially oak and beech, are suitable for deciduous trees, whereas pine needle mould is best for pines. A mixture of the two when used instead of peat will benefit the trees and is less environmentally destructive.

Loam A soil which is neither heavy and sticky nor dry and sandy. A good loam contains a proportion of clay, sand, humus and silt, and is both moisture retentive and free draining.

Maiden A newly grafted tree, usually only a year or so old, still in the early stages of training. Normally applied to fruit trees.

Mame bonsai Miniature bonsai. Sources vary in the actual definition of the size of mame: some books of Japanese origin state 4 in high, others 6 in high. The general consensus of opinion seems to be, however, that a mame bonsai is one which can easily be held on the flat palm of a hand. In Japan good mame bonsai are almost as perfect in detail as larger trees but in the West the specialized skills are only partially developed.

Matsu Japanese for pine.

Moyogi The informal upright style of bonsai. This is the most commonly grown style and has come to encompass many of those trees which do not fall comfortably into another style. The traditional Moyogi has a trunk which gently bends first one way then the other in ever diminishing curves, throwing out a branch on each outer curve convexity. In spite of the variety of shapes which are accepted (in the West at least) as Moyogi, the true classical form is as difficult to achieve as any of the other more rigidly defined styles.

Native A plant which is believed to have arrived in this country without the influence of mankind. Some very common trees such as sycamore, horse chestnut, and larch are, in fact, introductions to this country and not native as some might think.

Neagari The exposed root style of bonsai. Ironically this style is more commonly found in Penjing – the original Chinese form of bonsai – than it is in Japanese trees. The calligraphic and emotive quality of line offered by the exposed roots contrasts sharply with the more solid, mass-oriented styles popular in Japan. Although it is relatively easy to find trees with suitable root systems for this style it takes many years for the epidermis of the root to harden off and adopt the characteristics of the bark on the rest of the tree. Until this has happened the bonsai will not be successful.

Nebari The visible surface roots of a bonsai. Ideally these should radiate evenly but not uniformly all around the base of the trunk. They should emerge gradually from the trunk and should enter the soil in a natural manner. Nebari which all share the same girth and shape are just as incongruous as one-sided or crossing root systems.

Netsuranari Root connected style – several trees which all grow from the same root. The trees themselves may be individually trained in any style which suits the species and multi-trunk planting. Naturally occurring netsuranari are root suckers – as in elm or some species of prunus.

Nitrogen One of the three major chemical elements necessary for plant growth. Nitrogen is responsible for healthy leaf and shoot growth, but too much may result in over-vigorous, sappy growth. Nitrogen deficiency results in weak growth and small, yellowish leaves.

pH The pH scale is a means of quantifying the acid/alkaline balance of a soil or compost. The neutral point which suits most plants is around 7. a lower figure indicates increased acidity and a higher figure indicates increased alkalinity. Although some plants prefer acid conditions and others prefer alkaline, their range is limited to between 4 5- 9. Anything beyond these extremes is inhospitable to normal plant life. The addition of lime to the soil can increase its pH balance while it may be decreased by using proprietary brand products like 'Miracid'.

Phosphates One of the three major plant nutrients, phosphates are responsible for healthy and vigorous roots and also assist in protecting the plant against diseases. Chemical symbol: P.

Pinching Removing the growing tips of the shoots while still soft using the fingernails or, in the case of most conifers, by gently rolling the tip between finger and thumb.

Pollarding The ancient practice of cutting back all branches to the trunk every few years in order to put the long growths, which regenerate after pollarding, to a variety of uses. Traditionally carried out on willow and ash, pollarded oaks, wychelms and hornbeams are also quite common. The familiar 'mop-headed' willows lining river banks are an unmistakable feature of the rural landscape throughout Europe and beyond.

Propagation The increase of plants either by seed, cutting, layering, division, grafting or, nowadays, tissue culture.

Pruning The controlled cutting back of woody parts of a plant, either to promote new growth, influence the flowering pattern or to aid in the shaping. It is possible to style bonsai using pruning as the only shaping technique as demonstrated by the Chinese 'Lignan' school, sometimes referred to as the clip-and-grow style. The drawback is that your choice of design is limited by the natural growth pattern of the tree. However, it is not possible to style a bonsai without pruning so this should be one of the first techniques learnt by the novice.

Respiration The 'breathing' action of a plant. The process involves the exchange of oxygen from the atmosphere with carbon dioxide which is released during the convertion of store foods into plant energy. In effect the reverse of photosynthesis.

Sabamiki (see sharimiki)
Sankan Triple-trunk bonsai style.

The attitudes of the tree may be upright, slanting. windswept or any other suitable design.
Sapwood The living wood forming the outer layers of the trunk or thick branch of a tree. The sapwood consists of several annual rings and is the means through which water and water-born nutrients are conducted up the tree. Once the sapwood has outlived its usefulness it in effect dies and hardens to form the structural heartwood which gives the tree its strength.

Sekijoju Root-over-rock style bonsai.
Shakan Slanting style bonsai
Sharimiki A portion of the trunk of a bonsai which has had the bark removed and the exposed wood has been textured and bleached to emulate weather-torn trees in exposed mountain sites.
Sokan Double or twin trunk style of bonsai.

Spur A short lateral side growth which only produces a very short extension each year and usually bears the flower buds.
Sucker A shoot arising from the roots or the underground part of a trunk. Suckers often form a trees major means of propagation as with elms, and are always the most easy to root cutting material.
Tap root The main downward growing root of a plant or young tree. These roots seldom go down more than five or six feet. Young seedlings and nursery stock will have tap roots which should be cut as high up as possible without removing too many side roots before training begins.
Tender Describes any plant which cannot tolerate frost and is liable to damage or death. All trees sold as indoor bonsai should be treated as tender unless you are familiar with the species and are confident that it can survive low temperatures. Even so, no plant should be introduced to severe cold without a period of acclima-

tisation or hardening off.
Terminal Refers to the upper shoot, flower or bud. This can be either on the leader (main upward growing branch) or on a lateral or sideways growing branch.
Truncate
Describes a leaf whose base, adjacent to the petiole, is flat, giving the appearance of its having been cut.

Variegated Applies to leaves which are patterned with patches of a contrasting colour, occasionally pink, more often shades of cream or yellow. The unpredictable nature of this patterning and the general business of its effect make variegated plants unsuitable for bonsai.

Variety A variation on the species, either naturally occurring or artificially induced. Usually the variety differs in one respect, such as leaf shape or colour.
Vegetative Propagation by means other than seed. For example: cuttings, layering, division or grafting. Some plants naturally take advantage of vegetative propagation and even adopt it as their main means of reproduction. Elms produce suckers, crack willow sheds branches which root, and many tropical species send down aerial roots which become established and form new trees.

Whorl An arrangement of leaves or needles radiating from the same point as in the non-extension growth of larch and cedar.

Yamadori Japanese bonsai term for a collected tree.
Yose-ue Group or multi-trunk style of bonsai.

Index

Page numbers in *italic* refer to the illustrations

A

Acer buergerianum (trident maple), 25, 29, 72, *72*
    A. palmatum (Japanese maple), *19*, 29, 36, 43, 52-4, 73, *73*
    A. palmatum `Deshojo/Chishio' (Japanese red maples), 40, 75, *75*
    A. palmatum `Kiyohime', 74, *74*
acid soils, 41
adventitious buds, 37, *64*
air, 43, 46
Akadama soil, 46, *46*
algae, 43
aluminium wire, 66
American buttonwood, 17
anchorage, roots, 32
annealed copper wire, 66, *67*
apple, crab (*Malus*), 28, 57, 98, *98*
artificial lighting, 27
Artistic Bonsai Concours, 15
Arundinaria (bamboo), 26, 76, *77*
Australia, 17
automatic watering, 43
autumn colour, 37
azalea, 15, 29, 33, 36, 40, 43, 54, 62
    Satsuki (*Rhododendron indicum*), 62, 111, *111*

B

bacterial diseases, 43, 46
bamboo (*Arundinaria*), 26, 76, *77*
bamboo, sacred (*Nandina domestica*), 27, 101, *101*
`bar branches', 25
bark, 35
    buying bonsai, 24
    composted bark, 46, 47
    deadwood, 68, 69
beech, 29
    Japanese (*Fagus crenata*), 89, *89*
bitumenbased sealants, 60
bleaching deadwood, 68
blood, dried, 55
bonemeal, 55, 56
`bonsai soils', 46
boron, 55
Bougainvillea, 26, 78, *78*
branches, 34-5
    extending, 61, *61*
    jins, 67, 68, *68*
    pruning, 60-1, *60*
    shape, 25
    wiring, *65*, 66-7
    xylem, 34-5
bright sunny rooms, 26
Buddhism, 14
buds, 36-7, *37*
    adventitious, 37, *64*
    flower, 62
buttonwood, American, 17
buying bonsai, 22-5

C

calcifuges, 41
calcined clay, 47, *47*
California, 17
cambium, 34, 35, *35*, 37
camellias, 15

`candles', pines, 62-4
capillary action, 33
carbon dioxide, 36
Carmona, 27
    C. microphylla (Fukien tea), 79, *79*
Carpinus (hornbeam), 29, 43, 56, 80, *80*
cascade pots, 52, *55*
cats, 43
cedar, Japanese (*Cryptomeria japonica*), 86, 87
Celtis, 28
    C. sinensis (Chinese hackberry), 81, *81*
Chaenomeles (flowering quince), 28, 82, *82*
Chamaecyparis, 29
    C. obtusa (hinoki cypress), 83, *83*
China:
    history of bonsai, 12, 15, 16
    indoor bonsai, 17-18
Chinese elm (*Ulmus parvifolia*), 26, 115, *115*
Chinese hackberry (*Celtis sinensis*), 81, *81*
Chinese juniper (*Juniperus chinensis*), 28, *28*, 93, *93*
Chinese privet (*Ligustrum sinensis*), 97, *97*
Chinese yew (*Podocarpus microphyllus*), 107, *107*
chlorine, in tapwater, 41
chlorophyll, 36, 37, 55
choosing bonsai, 26-9
choosing pots, 52-4, *52-5*
clay, calcined, 47, *47*
colour:
    autumn colour, 37
    and light, 40, *41*
    pots, 52-4
`combing' roots, *48*, 49
compost, garden, 47, 55
conifers, *34*
    branches, 25
    deadwood, 67
    leaves, 36
    pruning, 61
    repotting, 49
    wiring, 66
copper wire, 66, *67*
Cotoneaster, 28, 57
    C. horizontalis, 84, *85*
crab apple (*Malus*), 28, 57, 98, *98*
crape myrtle (*Lagerstroemia*), 26, 96, *96*
Cryptomeria, 28
    C. japonica (Japanese cedar), 86, 87
cutpaste, 60, 69
Cycas (cycads), 27, 88, *88*
cypress, hinoki (*Chamaecyparis obtusa*), 83, *83*

D

day length, 40
dead branches, buying bonsai, 23
deadwood, 67-9, *67*
deciduous trees, *34*
    branches, 25
    pinching out new growth, 61, *63*
    pruning, 61
    repotting, 49
    wiring, 66
department stores, 22
die-back, 60
dormancy, 37
drainage, 46, *50*, 51
drainage mesh, 50, *50*
draughts, 43
driftwood-style, *19*

dull rooms, 27

E

east-facing rooms, 27
Edo period, 15
elms, 54
    Chinese (*Ulmus parvifolia*), 115, *115*
    grey bark (*Zelkova serrata*), *14*, 117, *117*
embryonic buds, 36

F

Fagus crenata (Japanese beech), 89, *89*
fertilisers, 33, 55-7
    foliar feeds, 42, 56
Ficus (fig), 27, 90, *90*
fig (*Ficus*), 27, 90, *90*
firethorn (*Pyracantha*), 28, 57, 110, *110*
flint, crushed, 47
flowering bonsai:
    choosing pots, 54
    pinching out new growth, 62
flowering quince (*Chaenomeles*), 28, 82, *82*
fluorescent lighting, 27
foliage *see* leaves
foliar feeds, 42, 56
Fukien tea (*Carmona microphylla*), 79, *79*
fungal diseases, 23, 41, 43
fungicides, 68

G

Ginkgo biloba, 29, 91, *91*
grafts, 24, *24*
granite, crushed, 47
grey bark elm (*Zelkova serrata*), *14*, 117, *117*
grit, *46*, 47, 51
group plantings, shape, 24

H

hackberry, Chinese (*Celtis sinensis*), 81, *81*
Han dynasty, 12
heartwood, 34, 35
    jins and sharis, 68, 69
hinoki cypress (*Chamaecyparis obtusa*), 83, *83*
history, 12-17
holly, Japanese (*Ilex crenata*), 28, 92, *92*
hornbeam (*Carpinus*), 29, 43, 56, 80, *80*
houseplant fertilisers, 56

I

Ilex crenata (Japanese holly), 28, 92, *92*
immersion watering, 42-3, *42*
indoor bonsai, 17-18
inorganic fertilisers, 55-6
insects, 43
internodes, 40, 61
iron wire, 67
Israel, 18
Italy, 18

J

Japan:
    history of bonsai, 14-15
    outdoor bonsai, 19
Japanese beech (*Fagus crenata*), 89, *89*
Japanese black pine (*Pinus thunbergii*), 15, 24, 28, 105, *105*
Japanese cedar (*Cryptomeria japonica*), 86, 87
Japanese holly (*Ilex crenata*), 28, 92, *92*
Japanese maple (*Acer palmatum*), *19*, 29, 36, 43, 52-4, 73, *73*
Japanese red maples (*Acer palmatum* `Deshojo/Chishio'), 40, 75, *75*
jasmine orange (*Murraya paniculata*), 99, *99*
jins, 25, 67, 68, *68*
Juniperus (junipers), 40, 54, 61-2, *62*, 67, 69
    J. chinensis (Chinese juniper), 28, *28*, 93, *93*
    J. rigida (needle juniper), 28, 94, 95
juvenile foliage, 61, *62*

K

Kenko, Yoshida, 14
Kiyohime maple (*Acer palmatum* `Kiyohime'), 74, *74*
Kokufuten exhibitions, 15
Korea, 18

L

Lagerstroemia (crape myrtle), 26, 96, *96*
leaf mould, 46, 47
leaves, 36-7, *37*
    autumn colour, 37
    buds, 36-7, *37*
    buying bonsai, 23
    colour, 40, *41*
    draughts, 43
    foliar feeds, 42, 56
    juvenile foliage, 61, *62*
    photosynthesis, 40
    pinching out new growth, 61, *62*
    scorching, 40, *40*
    types, 36
    watering, 42
    wind damage, 43
leggy growth, 40, *40*, 61
lifespan, 35
light, 36, 40, *40*
    artificial lighting, 27
    bright sunny rooms, 26
lignification, 34
Ligustrum, 26
    L. sinensis (Chinese privet), 97, *97*
lime, in water, 41
lime-sulphur compound, 68, 69
liquid fertilisers, 42, 56
liverworts, 23

M

magnesium, 23, 55
mail order, 22-3
Malus (crab apple), 28, 57, 98, *98*
manure, farmyard, 47, 55
maples, 24, 37, 40, 56
    Japanese (*Acer palmatum*), *19*, 29, 36, 43, 52-4, 73, *73*
    Japanese red (*Acer palmatum* `Deshojo/Chishio'), 40, 75, *75*
    Kiyohime (*Acer palmatum* `Kiyohime'), 74, *74*
    trident (*Acer buergerianum*), 25, 29, 72, *72*
Metropolitan Art Museum, Tokyo, 15
molybdenum, 55
moss, on soil, 23
Murraya, 26
    M. paniculata (jasmine orange), 99, *99*
Myrtus (myrtle), 27
    M. apiculata, 100, *100*

127

N

Nandina domestica (sacred bamboo), 27, 101, *101*
needle juniper (*Juniperus rigida*), 28, *94, 95*
needles, 36
   junipers, 61, *62*
   pines, 62-4
nitrogen, 55, 56-7
nitrogen-free fertilisers, 57
north-facing rooms, 27
nurseries, 18, *18, 19,* 22, *22, 23, 23*
nutrients:
   absorbtion by roots, 32, 33
   storage in roots, 33

O

Olea europea (olive), 18, 26, 102, *103*
organic fertilisers, 55-6
organic matter, soil, 46-7, *46*
osmosis, 32
outdoor bonsai, 19
   over winter *121,* 121
overhead watering, 42

P

Paris Exhibition (1937), 17
peat, 46, 47
penjing, 12
pests, 23
petioles, 36
phloem, 33, 35
phosphates, 56, 57
phosphorus, 55
photosynthesis, 36, 40
phytopthera, 41
Picea, 28
pigments, leaf colour, 37
pinching out new growth, 61-5, *61*
3
Pinus (pines), 17, 40, 54, 57, 62-5, *64, 67, 69*
   P. parviflora (white pine), 24, 28, 104, *104*
   P. pentaphylla (white pine), 104, *104*
   P. thunbergii (Japanese black pine), *15,* 24, 28, 105, *105*
Pistacia terebinthus (pistachio), *16, 18,* 26, 106, *106*
plastic-coated iron wire, 67
plasticene, 60
Podocarpus, 26, *26*
   P. microphyllus (Chinese yew), 107, *107*
pomegranate (*Punica granatum*), 18, 26, 108, 109

pores, leaves, 36
Port Jackson fig, 17
potash, 33, 56, 57
potassium, 33, 55
potbound trees, watering, 42
pots:
   choosing, 52-4, *52-5*
   repotting, 48-51, *48*
potting composts, 46
privet, Chinese (*Ligustrum sinensis*), 97, *97*
pruning:
   branches, 60-1, *60*
   pinching out new growth, 61-5, *61-3*
   roots, 33, 48-9, *49*
pumice, crushed, 47
Punica granatum (pomegranate), 18, 26, 108, 109
Pyracantha (firethorn), 28, 57, 110, *110*

Q

quince, flowering (*Chaenomeles*), 28, 82, *82*

R

rainwater, 41
regeneration pruning, 61
repotting, 48-51, *48*
Rhododendron indicum (Satsuki azalea), 62, 111, *111*
river sand, 47
roots, 32-3, *32-3*
   anchorage, 32
   breathing, 46
   buying bonsai, 23
   fertilisers, 56
   indoor bonsai, 24
   nutrient storage, 33
   outdoor bonsai, 24
   pruning, 33, 48-51, *49*
   repotting, 48-51, *48*
   root burn, 33
   root hairs, 32
   root stocks, 24
   watering, 42

S

sacred bamboo (*Nandina domestica*), 27, 101, *101*
Sageretia, 27
   S. theezans, 16, 112, *112*
sand, 46, 47
sap, creating jins and sharis, 68-9
sapwood, 34
Satsuki azalea (*Rhododendron*

indicum), 62, 111, *111*
scales, buds, 36
scars *see* wounds
scissors, 62
scorched leaves, 40, *40*
Scots pine, 17
sealants, wounds, 60
secateurs, 60
Serissa, 26, 54
   S. foetida (tree of a thousand stars), 113, *113*
shade, 36
shaded gardens, 29
shape, 24-5
   choosing pots, 52
   wiring, 65, 66-7
sharis, 67-8, *67, 69*
shoots:
   cambium, 34, *35*
   pinching out new growth, 61-2, *61*
slow release fertilisers, 56
slugs, 43
snails, 43
soil, 46-7
   air spaces, 46
   conditioners, 47, *47*
   drainage, 41, *41,* 46, 50, 51
   mixing your own, 467, *47*
   repotting, 48, 50, 51
   types, 46, *46*
   water retention, 46, 47
   watering, 41, 42-3
southfacing rooms, 26
specialist nurseries, 23
spider mites, 23
Stewartia, 29, *29*
   S. monadelpha, 114, *114*
stomata, 36
Stuartia (*Stewartia monadelpha*), 114, *114*
sugars:
   autumn colours, 37
   phloem, 35
   photosynthesis, 36
sunlight, 28, 36, 40
sunny gardens, 28
sunny rooms, 26

T

Taiwan, 18
tapwater, 41
tools 122-123, *122, 123*
trace elements, 23, 55, 56
transplanting, 33
trauma, bud production, 36-7
tree of a thousand stars (*Serissa*

foetida), 113, *113*
trident maple (*Acer buergerianum*), 25, 29, 72, *72*
trunk, 34-5
   choosing pots, 52
   repotting, 51
   shape, 24
   sharis, 67-8, *67, 69*
turning bonsai, 40
tweezers, 61

U

Ulmus, 28
   U. parvifolia (Chinese elm), 26, 115, *115*
United States of America, 17

W

water:
   absorption by roots, 323
   drainage, 46, 50, 51
   water softeners, 41
   watering, 40-3, *42*
   waterlogging, 46
waxy coating, leaves, 36
westfacing rooms, 26
white pine (*Pinus parviflora*), 24, 28, 104, *104*
winds, 43
wire cutters, 66
wiring:
   branches, 65, 66-7
   repotting, 51
   scars, 24, *25,* 66, *66*
Wisteria, 28, 116, *116*
World War Two, 17
wounds:
   buying bonsai, 23, 245
   cambium, 34, *35*
   pruning branches, 60, *60*

X

xylem, 32-3, 34-5

Y

yellowing leaves, 23
yews, 29, 54
   Chinese (*Podocarpus microphyllus*), 107, *107*

Z

Zelkova, 29, 52-4
   Z. serrata (grey bark elm), *14,* 117, *117*
Zen religion, 14
zinc, 55

ACKNOWLEDGEMENTS

The publishers would like to thank Peter Chan at Heron Bonsai and Charlotte Dalampira at Tokonoma Bonsai
for all their help in providing bonsai trees for photography

Bridgeman Art Library /Fitzwilliam Museum, University of Cambridge 13; Peter Chan /Herons 18, 19 bottom, 19 top; Corbis UK Ltd /Bettman 14 bottom
E.T. Archive /Victoria & Albert Museum 17; Garden Picture Library /David Askham 78 top, /Christopher Fairweather 82 right, /JS Sira 116 top, /Brigitte
Thomas 34 bottom; Colin Lewis 9, 35, 119, 120, 121; Reed International Books Ltd. /Peter Myers/Herons 14 top, 20 /21, 22, 25 bottom, 52, 53, 54 bottom,
54 top, 55 right, 55 top left, 55 bottom left, 72, 73, 74, 75 left, 80 right, 80 left, 82 left, 83, 84, 86, 89, 91, 92, 93, 95, 98 left, 103 , 104 , 108 , 110 , 111 , 114 ,
115 , 116 bottom, 117 , /Peter Myers/Colin Lewis 1 , 2 /3, 4 /5, 10 /11, 21 inset, 24 bottom, 24 top, 30 /31, 31 inset, 32 bottom, 32 top, 36 top, 36 above centre, 36 below centre, 36 bottom, 38 /39, 40 bottom, 40, 41 top, 41 bottom, 42, 44/45, 46 top, 46 bottom, 46 centre, 47 top, 47 bottom, 48 bottom, 48 top,
49 top, 49 bottom, 50 top, 50 bottom, 51 bottom, 51 top, 58 /59, 59 inset, 60, 61 bottom, 61 top, 61 centre, 62 centre, 62 top, 63, 64 bottom, 64 top, 65
above centre, 65 bottom, 65 below centre, 65 top, 66 right, 66 top, 66 below centre, 66 above centre, 66 bottom, 67, 68 top, 68 centre, 68 bottom, 69 top,
69 centre, 69 bottom, 70 /71, 75 right, /Peter Myers/Colin Lewis 51 centre, /Peter Myers/Tokonoma/Sandie Long 81, /Peter Myers endpapers, 6 /7, 43 top,
109, 118 /119, /Peter Myers/Tokonoma 23, 77, 78 bottom, 79, 88, 90, 96, 97, 99, 100, 101, 102, 106, 107, 112, 113, 122 centre right, 122 left, 122 top right,
122 bottom right, 123 centre, 123 bottom, 123 top, /George Wright 34 top; Photos Horticultural 43 bottom; Harry Smith Collection 98 right